Steve M

For your Success

Paul Bauer

877-937-2267

Over **88** Tips and Ideas to Supercharge Your Exhibit Sales

Steve Miller
&
Charmel Bowden

Over 88 Tips & Ideas to Supercharge Your Exhibit Sales

Steve Miller
&
Charmel Bowden

Printed in the United States of America.

Cover design by Ad Graphics, Tulsa, Oklahoma. 800-368-6196.

Library of Congress Catalog number: 96-95191

ISBN: 0-9655412-0-7

"Over 88 Tips & Ideas to Supercharge Your Exhibit Sales™" is a trademark of THE ADVENTURE OF TRADE SHOWS, Steve Miller, and Charmel Bowden, denoting a series of products and services, including consulting, training, audio and video-based educational systems, books, newsletters, electronic media, intranets, and other informational products.

Published by:

HiKelly Productions
a subsidiary of
The Adventure of Trade Shows
32706 - 39th Ave. SW
Federal Way, WA 98023

Order Information
To order more copies of this book, to get quantity discount information, or to get more information about Steve Miller and Charmel Bowden's other products and services, contact:

The Adventure of Trade Shows
206-874-9665
fax 206-874-9666
email TrdshwStev@aol.com
WWW www.theadventure.com

Other Books & Products

by
Steve Miller

How to Get the Most Out of Trade Shows
(book)
published by NTC Business Books
800-323-4900, 847-679-5500

How to Get the Most Out of Trade Shows
(audio series)

Stand Out in the Crowd
(4-part audio/video series)
Module 1: How to Measure Your Success at Trade Shows
Module 2: Selecting the Right Show & Marketing Elements of Booth Design
Module 3: Pre-Show & At-Show Promotions
Module 4: Post-Show Follow-Up & The Closed-Loop System

Supercharge Your Exhibit Sales
(audio/video program, plus workbook)

Postcard Seminars
(six-part series)

Acknowledgements

from
Steve Miller

Thanks to all the people who taught me to be an innovative and unreasonable man: Tom Peters, Brian Tracy, Danny Cox, Dr. Robert Schuller, Charles Handy, Patricia Fripp, Bob Pike, Shep Hyken, Tom Conley, Jim Carney, Dan Kennedy, Jim Walters, Jack Libby, Shirley Lyster, Ayn Rand, the Carroll Gang, Craig & Stacy Beaudine, Richard Branson, Earl Nightingale, Michael Murphy, Eliyahu Goldratt, and Michael LeBoeuf. If I left anybody out, please accept my apologies, and write in your name below:

from
Charmel Bowden

I'd like to acknowledge all the experiences I've had dealing with the fear of change, the politics of convention and the unwillingness to be accountable that have created totally ineffective and expensive efforts.

It is the sum of these experiences that has driven me to seek alternatives in the way I do business and to establish ways to honor the priorities in my life. I only hope that I can impart some of this knowledge to inspire other people to conquer "Mount Inertia" and move successfully into the future.

Dedications

from
Steve Miller

To the two, **way-cool** people who make all this hard work, long hours, and too many frequent-flyer miles worthwhile:
Kay & Kelly
(Hi, Kelly!)

from
Charmel Bowden

I dedicate my part of this book to my family (Mike, Chelsie, and Nolan) and to Steve Miller, because they all believe in me and encourage me to take giant leaps forward.

Table of Contents

Why Is This Book Important?

Have you ever been asked to work a trade show, and you're instantly filled with dread? Or feel that knot in your stomach, knowing you're going to miss something really great in the office while you're gone? Or worse yet, you can visualize the stack of mail and the to do's on your desk that will be there when you finally get home?

You're not alone. After years of working with exhibit staffers, the complaints about having to work at a trade show all sound a lot alike.

But that was yesterday. By the time you finish reading this quick tip book, if you really have the desire to change your results, you will have a big bag of tools to propel you to success!

In fact, by the time you finish your next show, you will be so jazzed about the results you will want to do another one ASAP.

If you're still questioning whether to read further, consider this. What other single opportunity gives you the chance to talk to more qualified buyers in such a short amount of time?

If you're willing to keep an open mind, you can learn how to work sales in the trade show environment and have the ability to crack open the golden egg.

Take this information as seriously as it's intended and you will help your company soar. You're the single most important element of your company's trade show effort. You can single-handedly make things happen!

It takes a change in these four areas:

Perception
Attitude
Expectations
Actions

• *Change your Perception.* Trade shows are not a waste of time. They are the single biggest sales opportunity you can have in a year.

• *Change your Attitude.* Decide you want to make a change. Help build a team that can go to the show and surprise everyone.

• *Change your Expectations.* Know why you're going and get up every morning taking the steps to make it happen.

• *Do the Actions.* Nothing happens without work. People can even over-plan and use that as an excuse to avoid getting things done. Follow all the good advice you've ever heard, and even if you only get 10% of it done, you'll still be ahead of 90% of the rest of the sales people out there.

It takes a certain character to accomplish ***big*** goals. You need to challenge yourself to do it. It doesn't come easily, but with practice and little successes along the way, it will happen!

Take a good look at the following list of the ten best reasons for working your trade shows, and then ask yourself again if you're ready to give it a try.

"You can have tomorrow what you want because you're willing to do today what other people won't."

Ten Reasons Why A Trade Show Is The Best Tool You've Got

You can:

1. *Get 50-100 qualified leads per salesperson.* And, we really mean, qualified leads. Not names ... but people who you have determined have the need for your product or service.

2. *Set appointments.* Be super-efficient with your time. Call your customers and prospects. Make a connection, make an impression, and the appointment is much more attainable.

3. *Build trust with your qualified leads.* Keep your promises. Send them the information they requested, call them when you say you will, and get their questions answered in a timely way.

4. *Demonstrate your product live.* This is a great chance if your company sells big things that you can't carry around in your car or on the plane. The real thing speaks much more loudly for itself.

5. *Strengthen your relationships.* Let your current customers and prospects know

you will be there. This could be your first chance to actually meet someone you've been talking to for a long time.

6. *Launch a new product.* Use the 'bigness' of the trade show environment to build on the excitement that an unveiling can generate. Get immediate feedback.

7. *Be right there with the competition.* The presence of competitors stimulates the buying process. Not to mention you can check out the competition first hand, with a minimal amount of work! See what they're doing so you know what not to do.

8. *Test market.* Get your customers' reactions firsthand. How do people really like what you're selling? Is the price too high, too low? What would they like to see? How do customers like to be serviced?

9. *Get noticed.* If you combine fabulous boothmanship with pre-show marketing and post-show follow-up, you will be in a league of your own.

10. *Do in three days what might otherwise take three months ... or more!*

12 Ways To Get The Most From Over 88 Tips ...

1. Exposition managers should send a copy to all their exhibitors. Corporations should send a copy to all their salespeople and exhibit staffers.

2. Assign **Over 88 Tips ....** to all of your salespeople to read in the next 3 weeks.

3. Ask them to write down the 12 best ideas they see in the book as they read through it. At your next sales meeting, have each person read his/her list.

4. Have your salespeople agree on the most significant ideas they got from reading the book and list them on a flip chart.

5. Have your salespeople prioritize the ideas and set specific timetables for implementing them at the next show.

6. Make **Over 88 Tips .....** required reading for every new salesperson in addition to your regular in-house training material. Design a 20 question quiz that tests the basic material.

7. Use role-playing to help your exhibit staffers more effectively open a conversation with a stranger and qualify them in under three minutes.

8. Send a copy of **Over 88 Tips .....** to the highest level sales manager in your company for his/her feedback and comments.

9. Design and post a chart showing the objectives and results of each individual staffer for each day of the show.

10. Look for your own tips and techniques and add them on the blank pages in the back of the book. Then fax them to The Adventure of Trade Shows for inclusion in future editions of **Over 88 Tips .....!**

11. Have a pre-show meeting immediately before your next major show to thoroughly plan your show strategy and tactics using **Over 88 Tips .....** as your guide.

12. From now on, before every trade or consumer show, scan **Over 88 Tips .....** as a refresher course for staying on track.

Reasons Why Exhibit Staffers Fail At Trade Shows

1. You're imitating the wrong behavior!

Even though you're reading this book, odds are you have worked trade shows before. Do you remember the very first show you ever worked? Think back to that time, and ask yourself a simple question: who taught you how to work that first show? The answer is, most likely - no one. No one taught you how to prepare for that totally foreign environment. Nobody explained to you the major differences between working out in the field and working an exposition.

Let's think about some of those differences now.

• You have only a short amount of time to interact with attendees. An average quality encounter at a trade show lasts only 13 minutes, barely long enough to introduce yourself out in the field.

• You have hundreds, even thousands of strangers walking by your exhibit, with the competition right down the aisle. Hardly conducive to an ideal private meeting with an important, new prospect or longtime customer.

• The buyers come to you, which can be good news or bad news. The good news is that large numbers of legitimate buyers can be walking the aisles of the show, more than you could possibly ever see in a few days out in the field. The bad news is that those buyers may be hidden by an equally large, or larger, number of non-qualified buyers. You've got to go through the process of culling them out.

• There are many more differences between working a trade shows versus selling in the field, and these are important to consider. But if no one taught you these differences and no one taught you how to work the show, then how did you learn?

• Odds are you learned by watching others. Other exhibitors and fellow staffers. Here's the big question, though. Who taught *them*? Kind of makes you think, doesn't it?

• After awhile, though, all the exhibit staffers start to look alike and act alike. We beat our brains out everyday to somehow separate ourselves, our company, and our products and services from the competition. We want our prospects and customers to somehow see us as superior in some form. And then we go to a trade show and blend in with the crowd.

2. Staffers have the wrong attitude.

The typical exhibit staffer falls into one of two categories. One thinks she is on vacation. "Oh goodie, we're going to Chicago! I can't wait to see all my old friends, go out to Gino's East for pizza and then hit Rush Street for some great dancing and music! If only we didn't have all those *attendees* we have to work with."

The second type of staffer thinks he's been sentenced to prison. "Why did *we* get sent to Atlanta? What did we do wrong? Why didn't they send Bob instead? We've got a lot better things to be doing than standing around this stupid trade show! What a waste of my time!"

3. Staffers tend to confuse busyness with effectiveness.

One major soft drink company called Steve in for some consulting work. When asked how they had measured success at previous shows, they replied, "if we pass out 10,000 samples, we know we've had a successful show." Unfortunately, this isn't unusual. Staffers need to understand the importance of setting clear and measurable objectives, and then develop a plan of action to reach those objectives.

Remember the old saying, "Actions speak louder than words."

CHAPTER 1

What Gets Measured Gets Done

So ... how do you go about setting some measurable objectives?

There are lots of reasons why people go to trade shows, some better than others. It's critical these reasons fit with your company's overall marketing strategy.

Trade shows aren't cheap. So, isn't it a good idea to know how the show can affect the overall bottom-line? And shouldn't the result be positive?

Here are some examples of measurable objectives:

-*Specific* number of new leads
-*Specific* number of on-site sales
-*Specific* number of post-show appointments
-*Specific* number of meetings with current customers
-*Specific* number of meetings with past customers
-*Specific* number of meetings with magazine editors
-*Specific* number of one-on-one demonstrations
-*Specific* marketing questions answered from customers and prospects.

Do you see a trend here?

Reasons Why Companies Decide To Exhibit

Generate leads
Write orders
Enhance their company image
Offer price quotes
Gather competitive information
Set up appointments
Do product research
Support the industry
Launch a new product

Exercise

If you could pick only 3 reasons for exhibiting, which would they be? You can use this list or create your own.

Now, narrow your list to two.

Now, narrow your list to a single reason.

The Point

All efforts at your trade show should be geared around this single most important reason. The rest of the list will come into consideration as you decide how to support your single biggest reason.

Know Your Objectives

Somebody once said (we're pretty sure he/she must have been famous ... we just don't know who), "If you don't know where you're going, you'll never know when you get there."

Make sure you know exactly what you're setting out to achieve by creating expectations for measurable results. Tie your intentions to reality.

Check in with your corporate marketing department for guidance. Know the company's overall marketing strategies. Then, pull the team together, and pick one thing that you want to get done at every show.

Don't let your mailers promote one thing, your booth another, and your sales pitch another. A trade show allows no room for additional confusion.

Remember, this is your single best opportunity to see more people in 3-4 days than you will most likely contact in an entire months work. Make it count!

ROI - The Magic Formula

The formula on the following page gives you a guide. Go through this exercise a few times and play with the numbers.

How many more leads would an additional staffer generate? Look at your closing ratio, your average sale or the life expectancy of your relationships. An increase in any one of these items carries a lot of weight.

ROI - The Magic Formula

Total Show Hours (A) ______
Number of staffers (B) ______
Total staff hours (C) A X B = C ______

Number of Qualified Prospects per Hour (D)
______

C X D = E
Total Number of Prospects for Show (E) ______

Closing ratio (F) ______

E X F = G
Number of New Initial Customers (G) ______

Avg Annual Sale of a Customer (H) $ ______

G X H = I
Total Sales from Trade show (I) $ ________

Life Expectancy of a Customer in years (J)
____

I X J = K
Total Return on Investment
from This Show (K) $ ________

Let's look at an example that demonstrates the power of these numbers.

Total Show Hours (A)	24
Number of staffers (B)	3
Total staff hours (C) A X B = C	72
Number of Qualified Prospects per Hr (D)	3
C X D = E	72 X 3
Total Number of Prospects for Show (E)	216
Closing ratio (F)	10%
E X F = G	216 X 10%
Number of New Initial Customers (G)	21
Average Annual Sale of a Customer (H)	$10,000
G X H = I	21 X 10,000
Total Initial Sales from Trade show (I)	$210,000
Life Expectancy of a Customer (J)	10 years
I X J = K	$210,000 X 10
Total R.O.I. from This Show (K)	$2,100,000

CHAPTER 2

Who Is Your Target?

Before you do anything else, you need to know the answers to these fundamental questions:

Why are we here?
How can we get the best results from this show?
What do we want to accomplish?
Who are we trying to reach out of the crowd?
Know who you are. Can you describe the company in 30 seconds or less to some one new?

In other words, know your stuff. The next few sections will help you figure this out.

Plan Ahead

Planning is critical. Pay attention to the tips in this book as you prepare for your next show. Each tip or idea you use will make a huge impact on the results you get.

As the saying goes, "plan your work and work your plan." Get your act together, whatever it takes. Because once you get to the trade show, especially if you've never worked one before, all bets are off.

It's time to work smart, because no amount of tips we can give you will make trade shows anything but hard work. However, hard work backed by good thought will pay off!

Don't procrastinate, either. How can somebody come see you at the show if they don't know you're going to be there? Attendees can only visit 30-40 booths. Shouldn't you make sure your booth is one of them?

"Only deal with what you can control, because everything else is reality."

A Trade Show Is More Than A Three-Day Event

We won't go into all the steps someone in your company should be doing before they send you out for a show, because there are lots of other books and tapes that do that ***(and we have those, too!)***.

This book is meant to help you understand how you can keep doing what you do best --- selling --- and adapt your knowledge for the particular opportunities and quirks of the trade show selling environment.

Once you get these things down, however, you may want to work more closely with your company's trade show coordinator. Together you can evaluate the entire process and make sure you're selecting the right shows, as well as maximizing the other elements of your exhibit marketing plan.

Know Your Show

Know what this show has to offer. Be prepared with the right product, geared to your target customer.

Is this a show that sees a lot of plant managers? Or is it one with an international draw, where a lot of upper managers show up? This will help you dial in on the presentation you want to make.

These days, a lot of companies are sending a variety of staff for input on the buying decision. You might want to respond to this trend by pulling together a strong selling team.

Remember, the best staffers at a trade show aren't always the salespeople. Your technician can win the confidence of a plant manager, too, or your shipping staff can hit it off with the head of purchasing. You may want to consider matching staff to expected attendee job titles.

A team selling strategy can remove your fear of the competition. If your customer has the perfect opportunity to comparison shop, so what? In fact, send them off with your blessing to compare. If you've done your homework, and your performance, planning and actions are top notch, you will rise above the competition. And, your prospect doesn't have far to walk to make his way back to you!

Know Who You're Looking For

Think of the description of your ideal buyer as though you were having to help a sketch artist create a wanted poster.

Bear with us here, and let's play this out a little further. You can't just arrest any person, you've got to arrest the right person.

It's costly, time consuming and wastes valuable energy to keep heading down the same dead-end paths. Not to mention the ramifications of a wrong decision. Rack your brain to make the picture come to life. The more detail you can provide the police artist, the more likely you're to capture your 'man'.

If the answers to your questions don't come readily to mind, go through your Rolodex for clues. Develop a profile for the people you're already doing business with. You'll be amazed at how much you can uncover if you review the facts with a whole new mission in mind.

Then go to the show and send out your *"All Points Bulletin!"*

Examples Of Your Target:

Answer these questions, develop your key suspect list, and you'll have the questions needed to qualify each person you talk with.

Remember, you can't arrest everyone for the same crime.

Questions to ask:

Are they the decision maker?
Do they have the job title you require?
Are they an influencer, specifier, installer or end-user?
Do they have the need?
Do they acknowledge that need?
Do they have the ability to pay?
What is the timing for their purchase?

These will also help define your qualifying questions which we'll talk about more a little later.

Know What Your Product/Service Can Do

The more you know about your product or

service, the easier it will be to garner the trust of your buyer. To refine this point, the more you know about your product, the better you can help the buyer.

Facts are good, pictures are better. From a buyer's perspective, he generally doesn't care how much stainless steel it took to build your latest, greatest machine. He just wants to know what it can do for him. And, he wants to feel it and believe it to the bone.

Romancing your product is an art form. So if the word "salesperson" still rubs you the wrong way, think of yourself as a storyteller. Try to understand what it's like to be the plant manager of a meat cutting line, or how it feels when the computer goes down. Or, the feeling of delight when your supplier is called about a problem, and you find out they can fix the problem on-line, causing only a barely noticeable blip in production!

Tell the story as though you're the buyer dealing with the realities of every day.

Know Who You Are: The 30-Second Commercial

Stop reading for a moment. Can you do a 30-second commercial on your company, its product or service, and your key benefit? If so, great. If not, we'd like to help.

Following is a template for how you can develop your own 30-second commercial. Fill in the parentheses with your information.

(Company name)
is for
(target)
who
(need/opportunity)
for/at/when/the
(product or service).

We are
(business description/category)
that unlike
(the competition)
provide
(what is different)
to/if/for
(key benefit).

Here is an example.

The Adventure of Trade Shows
is for
corporations who extensively use trade shows
who
need to improve the return on their trade show investment.

We are
a full service trade show marketing consulting firm
that unlike
other trade show consultants
provide a
100% money back guarantee
if
we don't deliver the results you expect.

Play with this and see how flexible it can be depending on who you want to talk to and what you want them to hear.

Education Counts

A little goes a long way. In fact you may even read this book and think, "Gee, we knew all that." Think for a minute and be honest with yourself. Reflect on whether you "know it" or "do it." As Steve's dad used to say, "There's a lot of difference between ten years of experience and one year of experience ten times."

It's always dangerous to not know what you don't know. Think about it. Where have you learned what you already know about trade show marketing, and who says *they* know what they're doing?

If you believe (as we do) that a trade show can be the single biggest marketing opportunity you have available, it only makes sense to pay attention to how a trade show really works best.

All it takes is you, some good information (like we're providing, we hope), and the willingness to be hot! A little education can go a long way.

Must Do Activities Before You Get On The Plane

Send Invitations

Studies show that less than 15% of exhibitors do any type of pre-show promotion. Yet, surveys show that people will respond to an invitation. Because potential customers can only afford to spend time with about 15-25% of the exhibitors at a given show, most of them make a list ahead of time. If you're one of the few who let them know in advance what you have going, you'll stand a much better chance of getting on the buyer's agenda.

Make sure to give the buyer a good business reason to come. The likelihood of a visit will increase substantially if you provide a compelling call to action. Remember, if you can get them to come to you, your job will be that much easier.

A booth with the right action will draw

them to the action. If you demonstrate ahead of time what your company does, it may be the only invitation a buyer needs.

Make Phone Calls And Set Appointments

Always call to follow-up on invitations. You will increase the chances of seeing someone at the show.

If you don't get invitations out, it's still important to make a call. Leave yourself enough time before the show to actually make a connection. Try 2-3 times to get a real live person before you leave a voice mail, but ultimately leave a message if you can't get through. Make it short and informative.

If you do talk to your customer or prospect, invite them to visit your booth, then set a convenient time to meet with them one-on-one. (Make sure to coordinate appointments with other booth staffers so the booth is covered at all times).

If your prospect isn't attending the show, tell him about what you've got going on and ask for an appointment anyway (you had a good reason to call, so you might as well move on to the next step).

Don't miss this chance to make your customer/prospect feel like they're getting special attention. People love to feel important!

Develop Good Giveaways, Activities, And Contests

Work with your marketing department to find appropriate giveaways. It's best if they are clearly marked with your company name and have a long-term use, because the item will serve as an ongoing reminder of your company.

Don't make the mistake of giving a totally unrelated gadget just for the sake of giving something away. It's just one more thing that can cloud your message.

Take care when you plan activities to generate traffic. For example, a basketball hoop draws a lot of attention, and your booth will probably be jammed, but don't confuse busyness with effectiveness. You're at the show to capture qualified leads, not to figure out which one of the thousands of trade show attendees is the best shooter.

Be careful with contests and drawings, too. If the fish bowl is out towards the front of the booth, it will do a superb job of collecting names. But you don't want just names, right? You only want the names of qualified prospects.

Just because someone took the time to fill out a contest form doesn't mean they're qualified. When using drawings, at least put your qualifying questions on the form and require they completely fill the form out in order to be eligible for the prize.

Put the bowl towards the back of the booth, so they're forced to cross the invisible electrified fence. "Unqualified" attendees will cull themselves out by not entering.

CHAPTER 3

The Silent Sellers

You've heard the saying over and over, "first impressions count." Let's face it. We've been trained to be judgmental characters. It's almost impossible to not evaluate what you think of someone by how they look. This applies to your booth, too, and how effectively it conveys the proper first impression. Yes, you have to pay attention!

Use Positive Self-Talk

This is part of the attitude thing. You might as well give it a try if you never have before. What do you stand to lose?

Set your goals, write them down, and say them out loud as though they have already happened.

"I am a brave, outgoing, persistent, knowledge-filled business booker, who's having a great time finding people who are thrilled to do business with me. By the time the show is over we will have set 50 appointments that will turn into $500,000 in sales."

Have fun with your statement. Wacky is good, specific is better.

First Impressions

First impressions are the sum of what the attendee experiences in the first few seconds.

1. Does your booth concisely telegraph what it is you have to sell?
2. Are you friendly and not overbearing?
3. Do you look the part? Do you look like someone who would be good to do business with?
4. Do you have a good hand shake?
5. Do you have a friendly smile?
6. Are you having fun?
7. Do you look like you're glad to be there?
8. Are you confident and energetic .... even after six hours on your feet?

Yes, people can make up their minds about you and all these things, in just a few seconds.

What You Wear Is Who You Are: Dress For Successful Visibility

Again, first impressions count. Here is your chance to really stand out from the crowd! Trade shows tend to breed conformity, not innovation or creativity. Exhibitors tend to dress alike, look alike, and act alike. It's the normal business uniform (for men, it's the standard blue blazer and gray slacks or dark suit and tie).

Because of this, everyone blends into the crowd. You need to ask yourself what you can do to be noticeable. For example, if everyone else at the show is wearing a business suit, everyone in your booth might wear matching golf shirts and slacks or even bright red shirts to stand out. Consider wearing hats, or even crazy uniforms. One of our customers had a circus theme, so everyone was dressed up as side show barkers!

Neat and clean is the primary criterion, but by all means, be comfortable. The day doesn't get shorter just because the end is near. Nobody wants to hear about your aching feet! You should politely listen to attendees complain and share your utmost sympathy with them. But you're invincible, because you chose the right shoes to wear.

What You Don't Say Speaks Volumes

Trade shows, without question, can be grueling. Ten-hour days on your feet in the booth, with meetings on either end of the day, are killers. Add on the tasks of smiling and listening and thinking and talking and ... whew! You pray that the boss asks someone else to go, because it just doesn't sound like any fun.

You can go with an attitude like that, or you can go with one that sets you apart from the crowd. Either way, you still have to go. With the right attitude, trade shows can be fun and successful. Otherwise, the trade show business probably wouldn't be the multi-billion dollar industry that it is today.

Lots of people are making money at trade shows and it might as well be you! You just have to want to do it.

The "Grandmother" Test for Better Booths

We love this picture.

If you can conjure it up for yourself, you will be miles ahead of the rest of the pack. You don't always have control over how the booth looks if it's being handed down to you from the marketing department, but you can try to make the best of it with how you ultimately set it up.

Think of asking a grandmother for help (or anybody else who hasn't been in the business world lately). When she agrees, blindfold her and then walk her up to your booth. Face her toward the booth and then whip the blindfold off.

Give her 3 seconds to look at your booth and then spin her around so she can't see it anymore. When she has caught her balance, ask her to tell you who your company is, what you sell, and why someone should stop in. She should be able to do it easily if your booth is giving the right message. If she hesitates and sounds like she's guessing and then gets it wrong, you know you're dead.

Your booth is your biggest silent salesperson. If your booth isn't working for you, it will be much harder to get people to even pause for that moment you need to catch their attention.

Just think about how **you** shop a trade show (you've probably been to one before just for fun with family or friends). You walk down the aisle looking right and left, knowing you're there to shop but not really wanting to talk to anyone unless something stands out that interests you.

You madly scan the booths for a clue, looking for something to catch your eye. Then when you've walked the whole show you realize you didn't find the company you were looking for.

So, think about it. What makes the show you're at any different for the people who are there to shop? Having a booth that screams your message loud and clear will help your qualified prospects find you.

Silence Is Golden

Somehow, in a sales situation, there just never seems to be enough silence (from the salesperson) so it bears emphasizing!

Have you ever heard the saying, "You were given two ears and one mouth for a reason?" Think about it.

Always put yourself in your customers' shoes and think about what you like and don't like when YOU are the one doing the buying.

You want people to listen to you, don't you? You want the information you're looking for, even though you may not know exactly which questions to ask. When people are shopping they don't always know what they don't know so you have to SHUT UP and LISTEN.

Listening happens best when you're silent, not when you're preparing the next best thing to say or running through your pitch.

CHAPTER 4

The Show Begins

The day you've been waiting for has arrived. Are you excited about trying everything we've talked about so far?

Hold Daily Meetings

Why wait until after the show to figure out how you did? Hold a daily meeting immediately before the show opens each day with your fellow staffers. Ask everyone to report how they're doing and compare their activity to show objectives.

What's working? What isn't? How can you improve on performance? What "victories" do people have to report? What show rumors are running around?

This is a great place to make mid-course corrections and re-motivate yourself and everybody else for the day ahead (a little food on hand doesn't hurt, either).

Create A Team Challenge

Everybody likes a good challenge. So put your best incentives to work and get everybody working together. Have everyone decide what will entice them to meet their goals. Challenge each other by individual, by team or by shift. Make sure the challenge promotes the realization of your goals.

For example: the salesperson with the most outside appointments wins $5 from all other staffers. Or the salesperson with the most call back lead appointments on his books gets a first class seat home and doesn't have to help tear down the booth. Or, the salesperson who generates the most sales in the first 30 days after the show gets a $500 bonus.

Just make sure everyone knows the rules and knows what is expected and they'll usually be up to a good challenge!

When You're Awake, You're Working

Trade shows can represent a few days "off work" out of the office, a drudge, or the best days of your selling life. So, we'll ask it again! Where else can you meet as many potential customers in such a short amount of time, and have the chance to meet them face-to-face when they are most open to new relationships? You have to believe in the power of trade shows and adopt the attitude of going all out to take advantage of this tremendous opportunity.

From your booth shift, to a breakfast, lunch or dinner meeting with a client or prospect, to adding on a day at the beginning or end of a show to get out around town to visit customers in the area. Making the most of every minute will give you weeks' worth of work once you get home. Create your own business building extravaganza!

This is not to say that a few coffee breaks throughout the day and a good night's sleep should pass you by. It's important to re-charge and re-focus when the schedule is tough. Accept this ahead of time, and give yourself a challenge to perform. If you work a trade show hard you will get rewards in return.

Be Ready When The Doors Open

Obviously, you need to be on time. Attendees are always lined up waiting for the doors to open. Don't you want to be ready for them?

What kind of a signal are you sending if your booth is empty? How many prospects will you miss if you're still setting up the booth? In other words, there isn't a single good reason to not be ready when the doors open.

CHAPTER 5

The Encounter

You've picked the first person to talk to, and so now what do you do? There are certainly some typical approaches, and then there are some others that actually work.

In this chapter, we'll try to walk you through the first part of an encounter. Of course, no encounter is typical, so it's important to have all of this in your back pocket. Being aware of this information ahead of time will help you mentally prepare, and you'll feel more comfortable once you're in the trade show selling situation.

Time Is Your #1 Enemy

You don't want to talk to everyone that comes along. Because you're friendly and approachable, this can become a big problem. However, you only have a limited amount of time to spend with people. And you don't want to waste precious time if they're not your target.

Remember what your qualified lead goals are. You can only hope to get 4-6 of them an hour, and you have to go through quite a few more to get there. This means only two to three minutes per person on average.

Save the highly effective 15 to 20 minute encounter for the cream of the crop.

Time Management Tip:

Go to the office supply store and get a supply of those little colored adhesive dots. Get the smallest size (1/4") in green, red, or yellow (or whatever color you want). Put one on the face of your watch. Then, every time you look to see what time it is, you see the dot. It's something you're not used to seeing, so it wakes you up and reminds you to ask yourself the question, "Is what I'm doing at this moment moving me closer to my objective, or farther away from my objective?"

If the answer is, "I'm moving farther away from my objective," then you need to get back on track.

Starting The Conversation

Sometimes the most paralyzing moment hits you when you look down the aisle, catch someone's eye and realize they are probably going to talk to you.

If this seems absurd because you're the type who is willing to lie down in the aisle to get someone's attention, you're lucky. Unfortunately, not everyone feels that comfortable about starting a conversation with a "stranger."

Remember that almost everyone is out of their comfort zone at a trade show. Even though as an exhibitor you made the decision to be at the show because it makes good business sense, a trade show still puts you out of your comfort zone.

The attendee chose to come, too, but stepping onto the trade show floor still generally feels like entering shark infested waters. It feels dangerous. And, we're not sure at times who is really the most scared. But relax, everyone is human. Hey, if someone is rude, you don't have to do business with them.

Just remember, they have the same choice too!

Speak-First, Ten-Foot Rule

So, we've determined that you must talk to strangers because that's probably why you're at the show. You want to find new leads for new prospects.

Our rule is, when someone is within ten feet of you, you must open your mouth and speak to them. Once you open your mouth and start a conversation, you'll be fine. Remember the old adage, "a job begun is a job half done."

Now What Do You Say?
The Moment Of Contact

After you've broken their "pace and gaze" routine, caught their eye and are ready to speak...

Focus on the individual first and break the ice. Treat them like the person they are. Come up with two or three questions that are comfortable for you that can help develop a rapport.

Remember, you're not necessarily here to close the sale. It's more important to build rapport so you can ask your qualifying questions.

As they are walking by you might ask:
- How are your feet holding out?
- So, what's been your favorite thing to see so far?
- I noticed that you looked into our booth. What caught your eye?
- The show's really big this year. How much have you seen?

If somebody walks into your booth:
- Thanks for stopping by XYZ Corporation. What brought you in to our booth?
- Thanks for stopping by. What caught your eye in our booth?
- Thanks for stopping by. What problem can we help you solve?

Think of introducing a little relief, especially humor, if you can pull it off. Something friendly and personal is better than, "Can I help you?" (Response: *"No."*) or, "How are you today?" (Response: *"Fine."*)

In other words, avoid at all costs questions that can be answered in one quick word. Especially the word NO.

Qualify, Don't Classify

They've stopped at your booth. You've been warm, friendly, and interested. You've put them at ease and developed rapport. It's time to find out if they are interested in your product now, or in the near future. You need to qualify them.

Remember earlier when you figured out who your best prospect was? Now is the time to find out if this person is the right person. Ask them if they have those qualities you've determined you want.

For example if you want to know:

1. Are they the decision maker?
   You could ask:
   "You said you were looking for a new hydraulic pump. Are you the only one making the decision or should we send additional materials to others in your company?"

2. How soon do they expect to buy?
   You could ask:
   "You said you just wanted to see what's new. Do you have plans for installing a hydraulic pump in the near future?"

3. What is the potential size of the order?
   You could ask:
   "You said you're looking for a new hydraulic pump. Would you tell me a little more about how you use the pumps in your business?"

You don't know anything unless you ask. This will also help you avoid prejudging an attendee. It can be very easy to convince yourself that someone probably isn't interested. "Gee, we couldn't catch their attention, so they must not need what we sell." Are you that confident in your telepathic abilities?

Remember, stick to business with your qualifying questions, because you don't know until you ask.

Get Rid Of The Lookie Loos

Not everyone at a trade show is your prospect. This is a tough concept for many exhibitors. But it's mandatory to the health and wealth of your trade show objectives.

If it's clear you're having a conversation with someone who isn't a viable prospect, be polite. Thank them for stopping by, and move on.

Sometimes this is easier said than done. You were just so darn nice they really don't want to move on and talk to anyone else.

You could say:

> *"Gee, it really sounds like we don't have a pump that would work for you. Thanks for stopping by."*

or,

> *"Boy, I think we could talk all day, but I know how hard it is to see everything in three days, so I'll let you go on your way. Thanks for stopping by."*

CHAPTER 6

Now They're Qualified

It's time for more information gathering before you move on to the next prospect. Remember, you're not trying to close the sale here and now. You're just trying to achieve mutual agreement on the next best step after the show.

Tip:

Use a standard lead form you can fill out as a record of each conversation. You can print up one of your own, or contact The Adventure of Trade Shows (fax 206-874-9666) and we'll fax you one of ours!

Listen, Listen, Listen

Knowledge of your product is a good thing, but be careful you don't get caught in the trap of talking too much. An interested, inquisitive buyer gives you the opportunity to take charge of the conversation.

Now is the time to continue using your qualifying questions to find out more about the prospect's needs and concerns. Spend a little time on your product and the value-added benefits of your sales and service as part of your questioning, but again, don't try to close yet.

A good next step is to schedule a time to talk further (another good reason to not tell all up front). It's important to know your product, but it's even more important to keep the conversation moving.

Remember, silence is golden. Too many booth staffers go into the old-school sales mode.... automatically shifting into "mouth overflow" syndrome. The key is to focus on gathering information that will give you the opportunity to personally address how you can solve their problems the next time you talk.

There are times when the prospect wants to engage in a more detailed discussion. Sometimes you can circumvent this by suggesting that the question is a good topic to discuss when you have more time. Sometimes you need to answer.

There are many benefits of being a good listener.

For example, a question about product durability may also be a question about your company's return policy. Or, a question about service may really be a question about product durability. You have to listen and carefully uncover what the issues really are.

If you try to understand rather than sell

you will generally be a much better listener. This, in turn, will usually give you much better information to get you closer to the sale.

Watch The Nonverbal Signals

This is not meant to be an in-depth study of nonverbal body language. It's just a reminder that you need to pay attention. Research has shown that the main way an attendee remembers your exhibit is based on the behavior of the booth staff. The long and the short of it is ... people intuitively learn more than they realize they do.

Look for any abrupt change in body language, and adjust for it with your prospect. It could mean the difference between getting the appointment or not.

Learn How To Summarize And Take Notes

You're going to be talking to a lot of people, so the practicality of taking notes is probably pretty obvious. The other good reason to take notes is that it makes your prospect feel important. That you're listening carefully enough to take notes sends an important message.

This is where a lead form can come in handy. This helps you make sure you ask the right questions for great follow-up. It also helps you keep your mouth shut and ears open. You need to be able to *really* understand what your prospect is saying vs. what you *think* they are saying.

An attendee's comment about equipment failure in their plant could be about the equipment itself, about their service department, about equipment performing beyond capacity, or about them not being involved in the decision to buy in the first place. You need to know how to summarize what the prospect is saying to you, ask for clarification if you don't understand and take good notes so you can address their particular issue.

Mutual Agreement

This gets back to the purpose of the trade show encounter. Let us give you our definition:

> ***The purpose of the trade show encounter is to get the prospect or current customer to agree to move to the next step in the relationship-building process, whatever that step might be.***

For example, maybe your objective is to actually write orders. Then, this is what you're trying to get the prospect to mutually agree upon right there. That's your close. You're asking for the order.

But let's say you're not there for the orders, you're there to get leads. Most staffers don't realize that once you identify somebody who fits your target market you have, in fact, accomplished your objective. So in reality, we need to think one step further.

Let's say, for example, you're looking for personal appointments after the show. That's the commitment you're asking for. You're taking them far enough along in your presentation and the relationship-building process at the show to get them to agree to that personal appointment.

The questioning might go like this:

Q. *"It sounds like it makes sense for the two of us to discuss this further. How about we set up a personal appointment? What is better for you, the first part of the week or the end of the week?"*

A. *"I don't have any time next week to meet."*

Q. *"We can chat by phone then. Which works better, Tuesday or Thursday?"*

A. *"Thursday."*
Q. *"Morning or afternoon?"*

A. *"Afternoon."*

Response and close. *"Great! I'll call you on Thursday at 2:00. How does that sound?"*

The prospect agrees, and you close.

If it doesn't go that easily and they don't want a telephone call, you may want to make sure you have qualified them correctly.

If you've tried booking a personal appointment and a telephone appointment and neither of those is doable, then you should at least ask if they would like more information in the mail.

Example:

"Would you like some information? Let me send it to you in the mail. I'll have it in your hands by next week, and will call you the week after. Will that give you enough time to look at it?"

This is all about getting them to agree to the next step. If they don't agree, they're probably not your prospect after all.

CHAPTER 7

Other Tips To Pay Attention To Win The Encounter

The following pages include more ideas about things to think about. Because an encounter is so unpredictable, it's hard to really talk about them in any particular order. Some are tips for selling, some are just mental health notes! You just need to be aware and ready to use when the situation arises.

Acknowledge Them Immediately

Have you ever walked into a room where you don't know anyone and tried to slide into a closed circle? It's almost impossible, and very uncomfortable, isn't it?

Have you ever gone into a store wanting to buy something and the salesperson is on the phone or talking to someone else, and you feel like you don't exist? What do you do? You probably don't wait long.

So, don't do this to people who walk in your booth! Include them if you can, or give them a questionnaire to fill out, or point them in the direction of something to look at in your display.

Whatever it takes, excuse yourself for a

moment and let them know you'll be right with them.

NOTE: This is something you'll want to discuss with your other staffers. No matter what the team challenge is, make sure you always have a policy to get to any customer as quickly as possible, no matter who welcomed them into the booth.

Don't Let Them Get Away

There are usually times in the show you'll be very busy, so you need to plan for them. Here are some things you can do:

1. Bring enough staff. Don't overcrowd your booth, but make sure you have more than one person whenever you can. This will at least mean the booth will never be empty -- a cardinal sin.
2. Have a video running continuously that can keep prospects entertained and informed about your services. Keep it short, though, about 3-5 minutes. People won't wait longer.
3. Have materials in binders for them to look at.
4. Have a sign-up sheet.
5. Get their business card if they look like they're in a hurry. Give them yours, too.

Make Attendees Feel Important

Every trade show attendee wants to feel important. This should not be a revelation. In fact, everyone you know (including yourself) wears an invisible neon sign that says just that.

"Make me feel important!"

They've come to the show for a reason. It's your job to uncover that reason in order to find out if it makes sense for you to consider doing business together.

If you think about the person instead of the sale, you'll have a lot better chance of finding out what you need to know (even if it means wishing them well and sending them on their way).

Don't Look Around For A Better Prospect

Relationship. The buzz word of the decade. But a very valuable buzz word. There is no doubt that the single greatest opportunity to differentiate yourself from the competition is to sell yourself. But you need to be sellable.

At this point you may want to review the Return on Objective chart on page 34. What the customer buys today is worth a whole lot more if you can keep 'em happy.

We all do things differently if we know we're in it for the long haul, rather than just for the moment. If you're not interested in building long-term relationships with your customers, maybe you're reading the wrong book.

You can rank your prospects as 'A' prospects who are "hot to buy now" to 'B's who are 90 days off to 'C's who are 6 months or more away. Just because someone isn't interested immediately doesn't necessarily make them someone to turn away hastily.

People buy from people they know, and from people they trust. This is the primary reason why trying to write orders at a trade show isn't always the wisest choice. Prospects can't possibly get enough information about you or your company in such a short amount of time. It's not about the literature you shove in their hand or about the fact that you are even there.

Prospects need to see some sort of proof that you're someone they would enjoy doing business with. Therein lies a great opportunity to follow-up with them so you can begin building trust!

People Are Naturally Skeptical

This is a simple fact. Unfortunate, but true.

People have seen one too many song and dance shows. Anyone can claim that their service is what makes the difference.

This is where you have to come up with specifics and do what you promise. If you say you're going to send it, send it. If you say you're going to call, call. If you follow through with what you say you're going to do you will be in the minority, and people will remember.

Always Tell The Truth

Don't be afraid to tell a prospect you don't know the answer to something. Offer to find out and get back to them. Make a note and follow through. This will show them you can be counted on.

How do you think people in used car sales got such a bad reputation? Because there are people out there who will say anything for a deal. Or, they'll say something because they don't want any one to know they don't know!

Be honest and do what you say you're going to do, and you have a great shot at creating a new customer.

Know Your RTQ

Rejection Tolerance Quotient. Most of us

know that it's not easy to engage in conversations with strangers. You will have plenty of people in the course of the day tell you they are not interested.

On the 1-10 RTQ scale, a "10" is someone who loves cold-calling. They have no problem with rejection. This person can literally stand in the aisle and direct traffic into their booth. Attendees pushing past don't bother him or her.

A "1" is someone who stands *behind* the booth, they're so terrified of rejection. Most of us are somewhere in between, so we have to be mentally prepared to handle this fact. After all, if our top objective is to generate new prospects, then we *have* to talk with strangers.

Remember, it's not unusual to take five times the number of no's to get to a yes. One thing we recommend is to celebrate every NO as one step closer to a YES. It makes thanking those people a lot easier. They just helped you get closer to your goals!

Never Underestimate A Prospect

Just because 99% of your customers are probably male doesn't mean you won't ever run into a woman who is your perfect prospect. The rise of women in upper management and business ownership virtually guarantees you will be doing business with women.

If someone is dressed casually, it doesn't mean they aren't a serious shopper. It may mean they chose to be comfortable.

And just because someone doesn't ask all the right questions doesn't mean they don't know what they are doing. They might be new or exploring or looking for someone to help them by playing naive.

You can't afford to pass judgments on people who stop in your booth. It's one of the main reasons behind having your questions pre-planned. Asking brings you much closer than guessing.

Remember: never classify before you qualify.

Badge Patrol

Where your own badge high and on the right. As you extend your right hand to shake someone's hand, your right shoulder also goes forward. This brings your name badge to the front, where it can be easily seen.

Don't forget to introduce yourself at the same time. You can also use your left hand to point to your badge, "Hi, I'm Charmel." It creates both a visual and audio impression. This is especially helpful if you have a hard name to pronounce.

Remember -- people love hearing their name, too! A name badge can be a great place for you to start a conversation. First, is the prospect a prospect or competitor? Name badges will sometimes tell. Then you can ask your prospect about their company as a way to start your probe.

"Hi, Terry. I'm Steve. I see you're from XYZ Company. Thanks for stopping in. What caught your eye?"

Keys To A Great Staffer

Following is a list of what attendees notice when they are walking the trade show floor. See how you stack up.

Attendees like exhibitors:

Who are outgoing
Who smile
Who are knowledgeable
Who are articulate
Who are assertive
Who are personable
Who pay attention
Who are helpful
Who are good listeners
Who are prepared
Who answer the real question

Attendees do not like exhibitors:

Who appear bored
Who complain
Who are overly aggressive
Who are too busy
Who are not paying attention
Who don't know their product or service.

CHAPTER 8

In Our Opinion

The following ideas are mainly good old common sense. But, unfortunately, common sense isn't always common practice ...

Don't Overindulge

.... on the plane flying in, at a hospitality suite, or out with a customer doing business. Why take a chance that you'll make the wrong impression or that you won't be your best in the morning?

Do all things in moderation. You need to be alert and rested at the show. Use common sense. You're not on vacation. You're at the show to get some big time work done!

Plan, Summarize, Sleep

After a productive day working the show, summarize your day.

- Prepare your status fax to send back to the office so they can get your info out to each prospect right away.
- Go through the cards you collected from

your qualified prospects, and make any additional follow-up notes you can think of.
- Plan for tomorrow and get to bed at a reasonable hour. No sense sleeping through the alarm and starting your day off with a harried jolt!

If you have any clout with your travel department, make sure you ask to be put in a room off the street, as close to the exhibit hall as possible. It will make it easier for you to maximize every waking minute.

If You Must ...

The following are things a lot of people do, even though we recommend not to. So, if you just can't help yourself, here are some ways to improve on a bad idea.

- *Don't have a fishbowl for names.*
  But, <u>if you must</u> have a fishbowl for names, because you are absolutely convinced everyone at the show is your perfect customer, put it at the back of the booth. This way people will somewhat self-select based on their interest level, because they will actually have to walk into your booth and risk talking to someone.

- *Don't have a magician just to attract traffic.*
  But, if you must have a special act going on in your booth, it really needs to somehow involve the product you're selling. The really good trade show magicians know how to do this. But we've cringed at those inexperienced magicians who are only there to entertain.

  The magician can magically make your product appear so you can immediately start talking about it. Make sure her story references the features and benefits of your product to help build the suspense. Think about it. Do bunnies appearing out of a hat really have anything to do with why someone should do business with you? We don't think so. If you do, call us and convince us. We're all ears!

- *Don't leave your booth empty*
  But, if you must leave your booth empty, make sure and have a looping video display so the booth can be working without you. Leave a sign-up sheet encouraging people to let you know they stopped by so you can get back to them. Or, have a special activity schedule for when you get back to the booth. Most importantly, think hard about why you're missing people in the first place.

Literature: The Expensive Crutch

Just so it's perfectly clear what we think about literature...

One of the most common sights you will see at a trade show is booth staffers handing out literature fast and furiously. Often the word "stuffing" comes to mind.

We encourage you to walk the show yourself. Notice that with just the smallest display of interest you will be able to collect bags of literature — without even removing your exhibitor badge. Most people won't even notice, and they probably won't ask. They'll just give and give and give. You end up with a pile of literature you don't need and don't want because you were just testing.

The same thing happens to people when they are "shopping the show." Think about it. When you pass out literature, it *automatically* goes into a bag with everyone else's literature. Is that standing out from the crowd or blending in?

Collecting literature as a buyer is an easy way of saying good-bye or walking away graciously. Or a buyer might think he maybe someday will have the teeniest bit of interest in what he thinks you have to sell.

If someone is truly interested, get their card and tell him/her you'll send the information. Then do it! This accomplishes three things:

1. It saves the planet! Just think of the trees you'll save. And yes, it also saves the cost of literature that really won't be used.
2. It forces you to qualify and get customer information.
3. It demonstrates you can keep a promise and be trusted.

Other Do's

DO show respect for everyone
You just never know who they might be.

DO involve the prospect
Get them to work your equipment if you have it there or get them to fill out your questionnaire.

DO put people at ease and establish rapport
Put people first and the sale second.

DO have plenty of business cards
Take too many. These are the cheapest thing to hand out. You can also write notes on the back, leaving your own reminders.

DO walk the show.
On one of your breaks, take some time to walk the show. Look at what other people are doing. Put yourself in the shoes of an

attendee and see what grabs you and notice what doesn't. Use the show as your training ground. And by all means, check out the competition!

Other Don'ts

DON'T ad lib

This goes along with telling the truth and knowing your product. It's always harder to correct a remark than to just not make it in the first place.

DON'T sit in your booth

The tendency is to complain about your feet, or read, or look at the floor, or smile at people as they walk by, or stare at the ceiling. When you sit, it tells people you're not interested, or you're bored.

DON'T eat

Again, what kind of message are you sending? Besides, who knows what you might end up with in your teeth or in the corner of your mouth? Have you ever watched someone else eat when you aren't?

DON'T smoke

Fortunately most exhibition halls don't allow smoking, but if you do it, take care that you don't smell of smoke.

DON'T cluster, hover, or stalk your victims
When you're in a cluster with fellow staffers it's darn near impossible for a visitor to break in. You want to do everything you can to be approachable. When you hover or stalk, people feel uncomfortable. You've crossed the line between assertive and aggressive.

DON'T complain
Attendees can complain. Exhibitors can't. Exhibitors even need to be sympathetic to attendees complaints. In fact, it's a good way to build rapport!

Some Attendee Complaints

National survey of attendees four top complaints:

1. Salespeople are too busy.
2. Salespeople are too lazy.
   This could mean salespeople are too busy talking to each other and don't appear interested in the prospect.
3. Lack of information and ability to answer questions.
4. Staffers don't listen.

Food for thought?

Never Imitate Other Exhibitors From Your Show Or Industry

This should probably be a lot farther up front because it's probably one of the most valuable tidbits in the book. So this is your reward for getting to the end.

When we say don't imitate we mean specifically...

Look at what everyone else is doing and then don't do it!!

Ninety-five percent of the exhibitors at a trade show have had no training. They've never read a book like this. So where do they learn? They watch what everyone else is doing. Big problem. Who taught those ***other*** exhibitors?

This is where you get exhibitors simply copying each other. "Gee, their booth is crowded. How come? Hey, they have a magician! That's what *we'll* do next time!"

Go back to your objectives and then figure out what to do. In the case of having a magician or some form of entertainment, ask yourself some questions:

- Is this something your **targeted** prospect would even care about?
- Is a *magician* the best way you can get **qualified** prospects to raise their hand and say they are interested in doing busi-

ness with you?

• Does a *magician* have anything to do with what you want a prospect to know or remember about your product?

• Is a *magician* the right tool to get them to stop and talk to you once the show is open so you can even qualify them?

• Will the *magician* help you collect names even if they don't stop to talk?

Now replace the word *magician* with any gimmick, event, giveaway, booth idea, attire etc. and see if what you're thinking stacks up to your criteria.

Once again -- does it appeal to the ***right*** target with the ***right*** message?

CHAPTER 9

The Day After

We know, we know ...... you just want to get on the plane and go home. You're tired. Did you do everything in this book? Then it should be one of the best tired's you've ever had. You should be satisfied.

Go ahead and pat yourself on the back. But don't quit yet. Remember there's still a lot of work to be done. And it begins now.

Do What You Promise

If you said you'd send information, send information. If you haven't already had someone at your office doing this for you on a daily basis, make sure you do it as soon as you get back. It's really impressive if your information can beat the prospect back home.

If you're not prepared to follow through, we can save you and your company a lot of time and money. Next time don't even bother to go to the show. It's that simple.

Here is your chance to exceed expectations.

Follow-Up

This isn't rocket science, so we'll never understand why studies from our office show that approximately 50% of exhibitors NEVER follow-up with their prospects.

What about the remaining 50%? Well, 30% follow-up with generic company information. No personal note ..... nothing. So this leaves about 20% who are actually followed up in a personalized manner.

In real numbers this means:

100 people were qualified and requested more information.
50 people don't receive any information
30 people only receive generic information
20 people are happy with the personalized information they receive.

National studies show that the average attendee has quality encounters with roughly 30 exhibitors at an average show. If only 20% of those exhibitors are following-up effectively, that's only ***6*** exhibitors!

Does this leave the door wide open for you, or what?

Post Show Trap -- Going Home

When you return, don't get caught up in the pile of things on your desk. Stay focused on the business opportunities you just created. Developing a plan before you leave for the show can be of great help to you when the show's over.

1. Extend the show one more day. Ignore the stuff that collected on your desk while you were gone. Use that first day back to handle the show follow-up. You invested valuable time and money to generate high quality leads. Follow-up with them immediately!
2. Remember those lead forms you filled out? Go back to them now and handle every follow-up. Plan for the ones in the future.
3. Recap how you met your goals. Get together with the other sales staff and finalize your challenges and make everyone accountable for what they said they were going to do.
4. Evaluate your success and make notes right now for what you can do better the next time.

Don't just fly home from the show and assume the business-as-usual mode.

Remember Who Fills In The Amount On Your Paycheck

If any or all of your compensation is based on performance, then you're in charge of the amount filled in.

Think about it. This is something you can control. You're accountable and responsible for the success or failure of the show. Your success doesn't depend on show management -- it depends on you.

Break The Invisible Boundaries

Think about the high jump. No one ever thought of going over backwards until Dick Fosbury did it in 1968. And look how records in all sports continue to get broken every year.

People train harder, they focus harder, they eat better, because they know what they want to do. They want to be world-class. They want to break the record.

This is the spirit to have when you go to a trade show. The trade show is **your** sports arena. This is **your** chance to be world-class. This is **your** chance to stand out from the crowd. This is **your** chance to break the records.

We believe trade shows are the single most efficient and effective means of building new business ...... if you take the opportunity seriously.

The bad news is -- the vast majority of exhibitors and exhibit staffers will never take advantage of the full potential that trade shows offer.

The good news is -- this presents you with a tremendous opportunity...

... an opportunity to create new relationships
... an opportunity to enhance current relationships
... an opportunity to recapture past customers
... an opportunity to generate great publicity
... an opportunity to test market new products
... an opportunity to showcase your company's new products
... an opportunity to showcase your own talents

and

... an opportunity to ***slam-dunk*** the competition!

You've got the book. You've got the information.

Go for it.

ABOUT THE AUTHORS

Steve Miller's innovative, results-driven exhibit marketing techniques have been written about in over 150 trade journals and newspapers, including *Fortune, Sales & Marketing Management, Success* magazine, the *Washington Post*, the AMA's *Small Business Reports, Business Marketing, Washington CEO, Medical Industry Executive, Exhibitor Magazine*, and *Expo*.

Author of the book, **How to Get the Most Out of Trade Shows** ($29.95, NTC Business Books, 800-323-4900), Steve's corporate clients have documented millions of dollars in revenues through the unique methods he's developed. An in-demand consultant and trainer, he has traveled over three million air miles and spoken to over 70,000 sales executives around the world.

In 1992, Steve led the world's first online trade show marketing seminar on CompuServe. To this day, it is still the most attended business marketing seminar in CompuServe history.

In addition to his consulting and writings, Steve has also produced a full line of video and audio-based educational systems, designed to help exhibitors and show managers more profitably utilize trade shows.

Charmel Bowden is known by her clients as "The one who creates the track to do the big things we have to do."* She has worked as a consultant with hundreds of clients nationwide to help them through the difficult task of doing business in this alarmingly dynamic environment.

The majority of her clients, ranging from K2 Inc., the American Egg Board, Edmark Corporation, and IBM have all significant investments in their trade show efforts as a part of their marketing efforts. Charmel has designed and built exhibits, staffed booths, created advertising and promotions, in addition to her staff and exhibitor training seminars.

She is a published writer and seasoned speaker who enjoys challenging conventional methods and demanding people set measurable objectives for everything they set out to do.

* Michelle Barry, Director of Communications, KCTS/9 Seattle

How To Contact Steve Or Charmel

For more information on Steve Miller's and Charmel Bowden's consulting, training, and educational products, visit our World Wide Web site at:

http://www.theadventure.com

or contact us via really old, traditional methods:

The Adventure of Trade Shows
32706 - 39th Ave. SW
Federal Way, WA 98023

Telephone 206-874-9665
Fax 206-874-9666
Email TrdshwStev@aol.com

Authors' Pledge:

No trade show staffer was harmed during the production of this book.